TOM LADUKE

520 West 21st Street
New York NY 10011

tel +1 212 445 0051
www.milesmcenery.com

525 West 22nd Street
New York NY 10011

PLURALIZING THE ACT OF LOOKING

By Benjamin Weissman

1. WHEN I FIRST SAW

a Tom LaDuke painting, I was shocked. Shocked on so many levels: genuinely floored, breath taken away. It was something I had never seen before, and it was astonishing to be in the presence of a painting that was unlike any other. I was not sure what I was looking at. It was seductive and extreme and complicated; it was a new weirdness, with a committed narrative, or anti-narrative, lurking deep down. I remember feeling a great joy in its other-language-ness—its range of voices, in all their inflections, shouts, subtleties, and whispers. It was a narrative of what I didn't know, and I loved the not-knowing. I was grateful for the right to delay clarity, to surrender, to give my brain time to process a completely new world. In that not-knowing headspace, I could start from scratch and piece together a fictional reality. And somewhere back in there was the mind of Tom LaDuke. Through his paintings, I might meet him, and what would that be like?

2. AN EPHEMERAL MOOD

It's all done with paint, but that seems difficult to believe. LaDuke's canvases often feature a base layer that looks like a gauzy, quasi-cerebral film projection seen through a scrim, a lacy nightgown, or fog. This foundational layer, this skin or memory membrane, is a dot-perfect, airbrushed environment, a montage of film noir stills floating in neutral spaces—muted, suggestive, disquieting, trapped, in a bubble. On other occasions, they are large airy rooms with industrial lighting, gray-white semblances of real life exhibition spaces (e.g., David Kordansky

Gallery, Gagosian Gallery, Galerie Max Hetzler) in a world populated by fictional sculptures. Establishing these nearly transparent fundamental layers for the paintings sparks memories and draws the reader/viewer deep inside the pictorial space. The inner surfaces frequently look like poignant flashbacks, an atmospheric gray bliss. It's LaDuke's way of setting the table, providing a straight man in a comedy routine, perfecting the stage for a comedy-drama that occurs in the foreground—BOOM, with an explosion of color, via animated paint splotches, swipes, blobs, dabs, rubs, scraps, meandering drips, writhing and swooping. It is utter mayhem, but really so hyper-controlled—a kind of double hallucination, one in black and white with elements of the real world, the other hovering on top of it in a vivid color onslaught, suspended in midair. This feels analogous to the way the best contemporary literature operates, combining a nonfiction "background" with voluptuous, fictional energy in the foreground. The backgrounds in LaDuke's work set up the big blasts of gymnastic foreground activity—activity that is a grand poetic intrusion, a stealth wrecking-ball ballet over the gray background establishment of a place. In my notebook, I found the phrase, *the image of an austere funeral home with flowers crazily blooming.* I envy a LaDuke painting's atmospheric gray bliss, its committed devotion to another world, its convincing arguments of controlled chaos and unreachable destinations, its laws of strange beauty. The interaction between the mummified grays and whites and the hyper-charged color bombs feels like the dead and the living talking to each other—or like the last image in your mind before dying.

3. PREMONITION

Tom LaDuke knows he will die on March 29. He is not certain what year. But nearly all the people in his family have died on this date. He and his brother call each other every March 29 to make sure that the other is still alive and to offer suggestions on how to survive the day. Stay inside, they suggest to each other, and then they laugh. The laugh is critical in the delivery. Ha ha. (Translation: Don't die.) It needs to be obvious that they're joking, even if that's not entirely the case. March 29 is written on one of his sculptures. That date's not going away any time soon.

4. GETTING LOST

on purpose is an important part of the artist/reader/viewer contract. LaDuke's work is a haunted house, a funhouse. He's brilliant at engendering a viewer/reader's imaginative surrender to his paintings—causing me, for one, to want to reorient myself into his world(s). Getting lost is so important here. Viewing these paintings means giving up your expected routes and sense of direction, letting the painting keep you off balance and giving yourself over to its vocabulary, layering, rhythms, rules, or lack of convention. What does the LaDuke work ask of those who are peering in on it? It's a complex contract. Patience, it says. Submerge. Look deeper. Let your associative powers flicker; let eddying connections swirl, bubble, and surface together—pop, vaporize. You think you're looking at something nasty? Did you make that up? Was it the red smudge? Are you both to blame? Are you on the right track?

5. THE PAINTINGS

can also be like strange parties: fun, interactive, loud, full of weird gestures and music. The flung look of the foreground paint brings to mind the astute ravings of a drunk at a party where unexpected things happen. LaDuke works a combinatory magic: the backgrounds and foregrounds interact to create an uncanny cocktail of reality and unreality. LaDuke messes up a painting in cool progressive ways that bring out new amazing associations. It requires the boldest heart, mind, and hand to pull it off. Messing it up for real in these paintings means that while the gloomy muted backgrounds suggest some reality we might know, the paint squiggles and splotches, the big wonky smears, and the reflections that appear to fly *in front of* that background, or *between that background and us,* seem like beings and events from another dimension.

6. IN ONE ASTONISHING PAINTING

three humongous wheels of glass vaguely connect at different angles. Perversely perfect light reflects off each round bar, suggesting objects and images surrounding them. LaDuke loves painting reflections, a visual high-wire act he excels at. In the piece I'm describing, the reflection contains images outside the picture plane that are too obscure for my brain to positively identify. These reflections are surrounded by various metallic shards and molten drips of lead with a small, intentionally out-of-focus portrait of a face, or faces. It is adjacent to a cluster of red, yellow, and blue bubbles, also alluringly out of focus. All of this hangs precariously, like bait independent of its line—painting as lure, as coy finger beckoning a viewer nearer like the best nasty dream. Oh, and there's a plinth in the background, with a head on it, seen in profile. At least I thought it was a head for the last 30 days. But now that I've put it in writing, I'm not so sure. I guess that's how heads are. They're oval, sometimes longish, and they have protuberances. This one has an oddly shaped brick for a nose—a stoic comedian's schnoz.

7. THE SPEED AND SPACE

inside a LaDuke painting is slow, molten, and taffy-thick. The backgrounds are a leaden, frozen moment, a hushed receding space, a deep theatrical site. It induces an illusion of dangerous, euphoric nightmare, a kind of pleasurable hell. It issues an eerie invitation to enter the gray-white afterlife. It's sometimes celestial, at other times deep underground, an airless crazy cave. When you get to the foregrounds of the paintings, there's a speed change. The paintings' foregrounds are a burst of provocations. Their acrobatic painting moves seem notational and intimate, a shorthand of diary-hieroglyphs, part of a dramatically completed painting. You can almost hear the cymbals bashing together in the orchestral pit. Like the Surrealists', LaDuke's world drips, redirects, mock-critiques.

8. REALITY

is present like a distant smell. But the predominant aroma in a LaDuke painting is an array of abstractions that conjure a cascade of associations. Reality, like the realistically rendered woodland animal, is a footnote.

9. ONE SCULPTURE

of a large white feather is made with hair pulled from LaDuke's arms and collected from his mother's head (via her hairbrush). The hair comprises the plumey part of the feather. The spine of the feather—technically it's called the shaft, that long thin bone that holds it all together—is engineered with fingernail clippings snipped from his fingers and superglued together. This would be a kind of mother/son collaboration. What sort of psychic tendrils are at work in this mysterious feather, and how will its potency steer LaDuke's future? What will it conjure? Everyone in their own little way is a warlock or a witch, grinding, stirring, simmering their potions. Everyone's got their private methods of communicating with things far beyond their reach. Like only the best of the best great artworks, the micro-laborious labor of this remarkable feather has gifts of its own, locked in the mother/son bond, special powers that began working the second LaDuke finished making it. The feather's psychic identity treads in the arteries of the ether. I found an old word today, cathexis; the concentration of mental energy on one particular person, idea, or object (especially to an unhealthy degree). Yet we know that what is commonly regarded as unhealthy is actually the only way for an obsessive to operate. And another thing: How does this simple feather change LaDuke's life? After the feather was completed, what prayed-for-things suddenly began to bloom? ∎

Benjamin Weissman is the author of two books of short fiction, most recently *Headless* published by Akashic Books. He teaches at Otis College of Art & Design and UCLA.

Belief in Giants, 2017
Acrylic on canvas over panel
37 $\frac{1}{2}$ x 30 inches
95.3 x 76.2 cm

Brave Distant, 2017
Acrylic on canvas over panel
64 x 86 inches
162.6 x 218.4 cm

You Are Here, 2017
Acrylic on canvas over panel
18 x 14 inches
45.7 x 35.6 cm

Object Permanence, 2017
Acrylic and oil on canvas over panel
45 x 61 inches
114.3 x 154.9 cm

Atonal Refrain, 2017
Acrylic on canvas over panel
16 x 16 inches
40.6 x 40.6 cm

Night Noise, 2017
Acrylic on canvas over panel
16 x 16 inches
40.6 x 40.6 cm

You're Not Alone, 2018
Acrylic on canvas over panel
67 x 85 inches
170.2 x 215.9 cm

Glass Altar, 2018
Acrylic on canvas over panel
58 x 95 inches
147.3 x 241.3 cm

Embers, 2018
Acrylic on canvas over panel
22 x 18 inches
55.9 x 45.7 cm

The Fourth Level of Worship, 2018
Acrylic on canvas over panel
27 $^3/_4$ x 36 $^3/_4$ inches
70.5 x 93.3 cm

Warp and Weft, 2018
Acrylic on canvas over panel
36 ³/₄ x 45 inches
93.3 x 114.3 cm

Silent Star, 2018
Acrylic on canvas over panel
72 $\frac{1}{2}$ x 59 inches
184.2 x 149.9 cm

Melt Into Stone, 2018
Acrylic on canvas over panel
82 $\frac{1}{4}$ x 104 inches
208.9 x 264.2 cm

Time Signatures Won't, 2018
Acrylic on canvas over panel
87 ¼ x 113 inches
221.6 x 287 cm

The Very Place I Could Not Remember, 2018
Graphite, CA adhesive, acrylic
12 x 8 $^3/_4$ x 9 $^1/_2$ inches
30.5 x 22.2 x 24.1 cm

Knights Meadow Marsh, 2017
Graphite on paper
11 x 14 inches
27.9 x 35.6 cm

Double Feature, 2017
Graphite on paper
11 x 14 inches
27.9 x 35.6 cm

Road Narrows, 2017
Graphite on paper
11 x 14 inches
27.9 x 35.6 cm

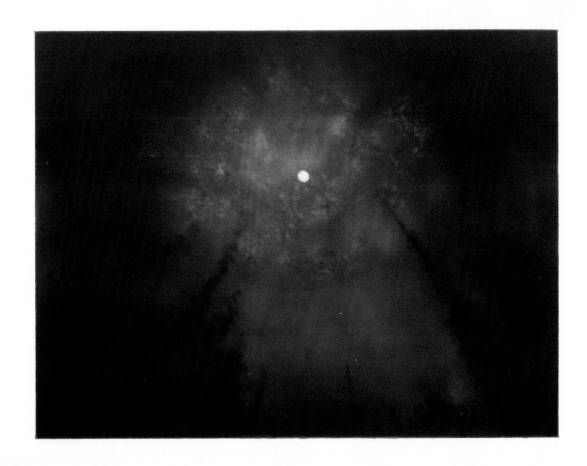

FLCKR, 2017
Graphite on paper
11 x 14 inches
27.9 x 35.6 cm

FLCKR (second version), 2017
Graphite on paper
11 x 14 inches
27.9 x 35.6 cm

Away Game, 2017
Graphite on paper
11 x 14 inches
27.9 x 35.6 cm

TOM LADUKE

Born in Holyoke, MA, in 1963
Lives and works in Los Angeles, CA

EDUCATION

1994
MFA, School of the Art Institute of Chicago, Chicago, IL

1991
BFA, California State University, Fullerton, CA

SOLO EXHIBITIONS

2018
Miles McEnery Gallery, New York, NY

2016
"New Work," CRG Gallery, New York, NY

2015
"Candles and Lasers," Kohn Gallery, Los Angeles, CA

2014
"Tom LaDuke," CRG Gallery, New York, NY

2011
"eyes for voice," CRG Gallery, New York, NY

2010
"run generator," Pennsylvania Academy of the Fine Arts, Philadelphia,
    PA; traveled to Weatherspoon Art Museum, University of North
    Carolina at Greensboro, NC
"Auto-Destruct," Angles Gallery, Los Angeles, CA

2007
"when no one is watching," Angles Gallery, Santa Monica, CA

2004
"Pattern Seeking Primate," Angles Gallery, Santa Monica, CA

2002
"terrane," Angles Gallery, Santa Monica, CA

2001
"Private Property," Angles Gallery, Santa Monica, CA

GROUP EXHIBITIONS

2018
"Belief in Giants," Miles McEnery Gallery, New York, NY

2011
"Loose Canon," L.A. Louver, Venice, CA

2010
"Inaugural Exhibition," CRG Gallery, New York, NY
"New Art for a New Century: Contemporary Acquisitions 2000–2010,"
    Orange County Museum of Art, Newport Beach, CA
"FYI-The Reflected Gaze: Self Portraiture Today," Torrance Art
    Museum, Torrance, CA

2009
"Tools," Alyce de Roulet Williamson Gallery, ArtCenter College of
    Design, Pasadena, CA

2008
"Like Lifelike: Painting in the Third Dimension," Sweeney Art Gallery,
    University of California, Riverside, CA
"New Works: A Group Show of Gallery Artists," Angles Gallery,
    Santa Monica, CA
"SceneSeen: Recent Acquisitions from the Luckman Fine Arts
    Complex Permanent Collection, 1979–2006," California State
    University, Los Angeles, CA

2007
"LA Bodies: Figuration in Sculpture," Angles Gallery, Santa Monica, CA
"Suburban Sublime," Museum of Contemporary Art, San Diego, CA
"Rogue Wave," L.A. Louver, Venice, CA

2005
"The Blake Byrne Collection," Museum of Contemporary Art,
    Los Angeles, CA
"New Works on Paper," Angles Gallery, Santa Monica, CA
"Terra Non Firma," Howard House, Seattle, WA

2003
"Sprawl: New Suburban Landscapes," Sweeney Art Gallery, University
    of California, Riverside, CA

2002
"2002 California Biennial," Orange County Museum of Art, Newport
    Beach, CA
"New in Town," Portland Art Museum, Portland, OR

2001
"furor scribendi: Works on Paper," Angles Gallery, Santa Monica, CA

2000
Angles Gallery, Santa Monica, CA
"Inventional," Angles Gallery, Santa Monica, CA

TEACHING

2010
ArtCenter College of Design, Pasadena, CA

2005
Occidental College, Los Angeles, CA

AWARDS

2011
Peter S. Reed Foundation Grant

1992
Trustee Merit Scholarship, The School of the Art Institute of Chicago

COLLECTIONS

Albright-Knox Art Gallery, Buffalo, NY

The Alfond Collection of Contemporary Art at Rollins College,
    Cornell Fine Arts Museum, Winter Park, FL

Solomon R. Guggenheim Museum, New York, NY

Luckman Gallery, California State University, Los Angeles, CA

Minnesota Museum of American Art, St. Paul, MN

Museum of Contemporary Art, Los Angeles, CA

Museum of Contemporary Art, San Diego, CA

Nerman Museum of Contemporary Art, Overland Park, KS

Orange County Museum of Art, Newport Beach, CA

Pennsylvania Academy of the Fine Arts, Philadelphia, PA

Portland Art Museum, Portland, OR

The Speed Art Museum, Louisville, KY

Colección Jumex, Mexico City, Mexico.

Published on the occasion of the exhibition

TOM LADUKE

15 November – 22 December 2018

Miles McEnery Gallery
525 West 22nd Street
New York NY 10011

tel +1 212 445 0051
www.milesmcenery.com

Photography by
Christopher Burke Studio, New York, NY
Robert Wedemeyer, Los Angeles, CA

Catalogue designed by
HHA Design, New York, NY

ISBN: 978-1-949327-02-1

Cover: *Silent Star* (detail), 2018

MILES
McENERY
GALLERY